MIX
Papier aus verantwortungsvollen Quellen
Paper from responsible sources
FSC® C105338

Sujeeta Sharma

Production Economics and Marketing Performance of Coffee in Parbat, Nepal

Anchor Academic
Publishing

Sharma, Sujeeta: Production Economics and Marketing Performance of Coffee in Parbat, Nepal, Hamburg, Anchor Academic Publishing 2016

Buch-ISBN: 978-3-96067-096-4
PDF-eBook-ISBN: 978-3-96067-596-9
Druck/Herstellung: Anchor Academic Publishing, Hamburg, 2016

Bibliografische Information der Deutschen Nationalbibliothek:
Die Deutsche Nationalbibliothek verzeichnet diese Publikation in der Deutschen Nationalbibliografie; detaillierte bibliografische Daten sind im Internet über http://dnb.d-nb.de abrufbar.

Bibliographical Information of the German National Library:
The German National Library lists this publication in the German National Bibliography. Detailed bibliographic data can be found at: http://dnb.d-nb.de

All rights reserved. This publication may not be reproduced, stored in a retrieval system or transmitted, in any form or by any means, electronic, mechanical, photocopying, recording or otherwise, without the prior permission of the publishers.

Das Werk einschließlich aller seiner Teile ist urheberrechtlich geschützt. Jede Verwertung außerhalb der Grenzen des Urheberrechtsgesetzes ist ohne Zustimmung des Verlages unzulässig und strafbar. Dies gilt insbesondere für Vervielfältigungen, Übersetzungen, Mikroverfilmungen und die Einspeicherung und Bearbeitung in elektronischen Systemen.

Die Wiedergabe von Gebrauchsnamen, Handelsnamen, Warenbezeichnungen usw. in diesem Werk berechtigt auch ohne besondere Kennzeichnung nicht zu der Annahme, dass solche Namen im Sinne der Warenzeichen- und Markenschutz-Gesetzgebung als frei zu betrachten wären und daher von jedermann benutzt werden dürften.

Die Informationen in diesem Werk wurden mit Sorgfalt erarbeitet. Dennoch können Fehler nicht vollständig ausgeschlossen werden und die Diplomica Verlag GmbH, die Autoren oder Übersetzer übernehmen keine juristische Verantwortung oder irgendeine Haftung für evtl. verbliebene fehlerhafte Angaben und deren Folgen.

Alle Rechte vorbehalten

© Anchor Academic Publishing, Imprint der Diplomica Verlag GmbH
Hermannstal 119k, 22119 Hamburg
http://www.diplomica-verlag.de, Hamburg 2016
Printed in Germany

TABLE OF CONTENTS

Title	Page
LIST OF TABLES	4
LIST OF FIGURES	5
ACRONYMS	6
EQUIVALENTS	7
ABSTRACT	8

1 INTRODUCTION 9
   1.1 Background of the study 9
   1.2 Statement of problem 10
   1.3 Research rationale 11
   1.4 Objectives 11
   1.5 Scope and limitation of the study 12

2 LITERATURE REVIEW 13
   2.1 Coffee in Nepal 13
   2.2 Worldwide Coffee production Scenario 13
   2.3 Coffee production in Parbat 14
   2.4 Economics of Coffee production 14
   2.5 Constraints of coffee production and marketing 14
   2.6 Market, marketing system and status of coffee 15
   2.7 Institutional involvement in Coffee sector 15

3 RESEARCH METHODOLOGY 17

3.1 Selection of the study area 17
3.2 Sampling procedure and selection of the respondent 18
3.2.1 Sampling method 18
3.2.2 Defining the population 18
3.2.3 Sampling frame, sample size and sample selection procedure 18
3.3 Methods and techniques of data collection 18
3.3.1 Sources of information 18
3.4 Survey design and data collection procedure 19
3.4.1 Reconnaissance Survey 19
3.4.2 Interview schedule design 19
3.4.3 Pre-testing of interview schedule 19
3.4.4 Field survey 19
3.5 Methods and techniques of data analysis 20
3.5.1 Quantitative data analysis 20
3.6 Economics of coffee production 20
3.6.1 Cost of coffee production 20
3.6.2 Gross margin, profitability and cost-benefit analysis 21
3.6.3 Production function analysis 21
3.6.4 Return to Scale Analysis 22
3.7 Contribution of coffee production in household income 22
3.8 Analysis of problems associated with production and marketing of Coffee 23

4 RESULTS AND DISCUSSION 24

4.1 Socio-economic and demographic information 24
4.1.1 Age distribution of respondents and household head 24
4.1.2 Family type and family size 24

4.1.3 Ethnicity of the respondents 26

4.1.4 Age distribution of the sampled population and their major occupation. 26

4.1.5 Educational status of sampled households 26

4.2 Farm characteristics 27

4.2.1 Land holding characteristics 27

4.3 Institutional characteristics 27

4.3.1 Organizational participation and Access of credit 27

4.3.2 Participation on trainings 28

4.4 Production economics of Coffee 29

4.4.1 Contribution of coffee in household income 29

4.4.2 Gross margin, profitability index and benefit-cost analysis on coffee production 29

4.4.3 Factors affecting the production of coffee 30

4.4.4 Return to Scale 31

4.5 Reasons for the cultivation of coffee 31

4.6 Constraints in production and marketing of Coffee 31

4.7 Marketing system and Marketing Channel of coffee 32

5 SUMMARY AND CONCLUSION 34

5.1 Summary 34

5.2 Conclusion 35

5.3 Recommendations 36

5.4 Areas for further research 37

LITERATURE CITED 38

LIST OF TABLES

Table		Page
1	Age distribution of respondents and household head in the study area (2014)	24
2	Distribution of the population by sex in the study area (2014)	25
3	Sex distribution of the household head in the study area (2014)	25
4	Ethnic composition of respondents in study area (2014)	26
5	Age distribution of the sampled population in the study area (2014)	26
6	Farm characteristics of the respondents in the study area (2014)	27
7	Organizational participation of Coffee growers in the study area (2014)	28
8	Major source of household income in the study area (2014)	29
9	Gross margin, profitability and benefit-cost from coffee in the study area (2014)	30
10	Estimated coefficients for the factors affecting production of coffee in the study area (2014)	30
11	Reasons for the cultivation of coffee in the study area (2014)	31
12	Constraints in production and marketing of coffee in the study area (2014)	31

LIST OF FIGURES

Figure		Page
1	Map of Nepal showing Parbat District (Research site)	17
2	Family type of the respondents in the study area (2014)	25
3	Educational status of sampled household in the study area (2014)	27
4	Training received situation among sampled households in the study area (2014)	28
5	Marketing channel of coffee in Parvat district (2014)	32

ACRONYMS

%	Percent
APP	Agriculture Perspective Plan
CDOs	Community Development Organizations
DADO	District Agriculture Development Office
DDC	District Development Committee
FGD	Focus Group Discussion
GFI	Gross Farm Income
GM	Gross Margin
ha	Hectare
HH	Household
IAAS	Institute of Agriculture and Animal Sciences
INGO	International Non-Governmental Organization
Kg	Kilogram
MoAD	Ministry of Agriculture and Development
mt.	metric ton
NGO	Non Governmental Organization
NRs	Nepalese Rupees
P-value	Probability Value
qtl	Quintal
R	Coefficient of multiple correlation
R^2	coefficient of multiple determination
RTS	Return to Scale
SPSS	Statistical Package for Social Science

EQUIVALENTS

Months

Nepali Calendar **Gregorian Calendar**

Nepali	Gregorian
Baisakh	Mid April – Mid May
Jestha	Mid May – Mid June
Ashad	Mid June – Mid July
Shrawan	Mid July – Mid August
Bhadra	Mid August – Mid September
Aswin	Mid September – Mid October
Kartik	Mid October – Mid November
Mangsir	Mid November – Mid December
Poush	Mid December – Mid January
Magh	Mid January – Mid February
Falgun	Mid February – Mid March
Chaitra	Mid March – Mid April

Area

1 Kattha = 20 Dhur
1 Bigha = 20 Kattha = 13.31 Ropani = 0.68 Hectares
1 Hectare = 30 Kattha = 19.66 Ropani

Weight

1 Ton = 10 Quintals = 1000 kg

Currency (as of 25 August, 2014)

Euro (€) 1 = 127.74 NRs. (Buying rate)
US$ 1 = 96.45 NRs. (Buying rate)

ABSTRACT

Coffee is one of the important cash generative crops in the mid hill regions of Nepal. Study considered the production economics along with marketing performance of coffee in Pakuwa VDC of Parbat district, Nepal. Survey was done in June 2014. Data collection was conducted through semi-structured pre-tested questionnaire administered on 40 farmer respondents selected randomly. Gross margin analysis, profitability index and the benefit-cost ratio (B-C ratio) was used to analyze the production economics of coffee in the study area. The results revealed that, coffee cultivation is a profitable enterprise in the study area. This is reflected by the gross margin of NRs. 90205.43 per hectare, benefit-cost ratio of 3.84 and profitability index of 1.23. Coffee sector alone contributed 16.26 percent of total household income showing positive sign for commercialization. The number of productive plant and cost on sapling were the most significant factor affecting production of coffee in the study area and holding the other explanatory variables constant, one percent change would increase the yield of coffee by 0.894 and 0.151 percent respectively. Further, increasing return to scale was observed in coffee production with value 1.26. Farmers explained more income from coffee and easy to sell as the reasons for its cultivation. Lack of irrigation and lack of detailed knowledge were ranked as severe production problems whereas; low price and lack of processing facility stood as marketing constraints in the study area. Study resulted positive economic significance of coffee and this shows immense need of Government, NGOs, traders, and other line agencies to lay efforts on production and marketing management such that its production and income can be raised.

1 INTRODUCTION

1.1 Background of the study

Nepal lies between $26^{0}22"$North-$30^{0}27"$North latitudes, and $80^{0}04"$East- $88^{0}12"$East longitudes with total area of 1, 47,181 sq. Km. A large number of people have the agriculture as the major occupation in Nepal, 65.6 percent of total economically active population is involved in agriculture (MoAD, 2013). Agriculture as the sector wise shares the 35.11% to the total GDP of the country. From terai to high hills, Nepal possesses huge potentiality of different vegetable, fruits, cash crops, medicinal and aromatic plants. High value cash crops such as coffee show great potentiality from the perspective of trade.

Coffee which falls under Rubiaceae family and genus *Coffea*, has two major species C. *Arabica* and C. *robusta* and one minor species C. *liberica*. As the climate and soil in the mid and high hills of Nepal are found to be very suitable for Arabica coffee, the coffee planted in Nepal is all Arabica (Giri, 2006). Coffee is one of the important cash generative crops in the mid hill regions of Nepal. Initially, coffee spread to several districts through the initiation of individual farmers as well as by an ADB/N supported programs. Presently, coffee is cultivated in around 40 districts, but it has been producing commercially in about 20-22 hill districts. Some districts like Gulmi, Palpa, Argakhanchi, Lalitpur, Tanahu, Kavre, Sindhupalchowk, Lamjung, Kaski, Gorkha, Syangja, Parbat, Baglung are successfully growing and producing Coffee beans and is increasing gradually (NTCDB, 2014). Coffees are mainly grown in the mid hill region of Nepal and is high value cash generating crop for hill farmers (khanal, 2003). Total area and production coffee in Parbat district is 76 ha. and 10.5 metric ton respectively with approximate 1800 farmers (MoAD, 2013). Whereas; total national area, production and farmers of coffee sector is 1750 ha, 366 mt. and 27000 farmers respectively (MoAD, 2013). Coffee provides 5 times more yield than that of maize and millets and 2-3 times more yield than that of any other cash crops (Dhakal, 2004). Especially Nepalese coffee has high demand in Japan, America, South Korea, Germany and the Netherlands. However, in comparison with demand in the international market, Nepalese coffee has low production and below the standard quality specified by the developed countries. Nepal has a great potential to produce organic coffee by utilizing its long back production system called as organic by default. Coffee is grown with shade crops of multipurpose tree species. It could be an important means for the soil conservation; biodiversity maintenance and watershed balance in the mid-hills of Nepal (Nepal, 2006).

1.2 Statement of problem

Coffee is a relatively new cash crop started to be grown in Nepal almost with no use of inorganic fertilizer and pesticide. It could be an important occupation in the rural economies with massive participation of marginal, poor and down trodden class of rural communities. In addition, it could be an important means for soil conservation, bio-diversity maintenance and watershed balance in the mid-hills of Nepal (AEC, 2006).

Despite the higher economical importance of coffee it is being devalued and graded as low grade agriculture product in Nepal due to the wrong and narrow conception of the people. Farmers are not properly and adequately aware of coffee farming technologies. Professionalism and commercialization have yet to be cultivated. The economics of production along with market and price information about coffee is not easily available and price is not communicated to producers until the day of trade. There is no proper market channel of selling coffee in local as well as national market. The mistrust and non-transparent nature of the pricing process, control of few dominant buyers in pricing and marketing, irregularity in the demand from final buyers/processors, lack of knowledge on the producer level are the main causes for information gaps. Thus the research on this study will become a fruitful for the economics of cultivation and marketing performance of high value cash crops, mostly in coffee production and its marketing potentiality for domestic and export market promotion. Thus, realizing this importance of documentation, production economics and marketing performance of coffee, this study is proposed to dig out promotion, support, extension of benefits along with marketing channels and problems. Based on this study a possible solution measures for promotion and dissemination strategy of coffee farming may be suggested. Based on the above statements following research questions were formulated;

- What are the gross margin, cost and benefit of coffee plantation?
- Is the coffee plantation profitable?
- What are the factors affecting in coffee production?
- What are the major constraints of coffee production and marketing?
- Which type of marketing channel is used in the trade of coffee?

1.3 Research rationale

Coffee is a high value low volume cash crop. National long-term perspective has given priority in high value cash crop (APP 1995).This crop is economically more (nearly three times) profitable in the present context as compared to other cereal crops (Bajracharya, 2003). By utilizing the comparative resource advantage, Nepal would compete for quality coffee production. However the volume of production and associated production cost accompanied with the marketing management is the most important prerequisite to be a competitive in the international market. Positive view of government on use of marginal land, cultivation can be done in marginal land, natural forest/ biodiversity conservation / soil erosion, involvement of marginalized people in collection and harvesting. Organic coffee production provides income to people with limited alternative employment opportunities and low income.

Information about prevailing growing and marketing system of organic coffee provides basis for the formulation of appropriate policy and act. Suitable policy will provide production and marketing incentives for this crop, which is on behalf of large numbers of rural poor farmer living in mid-hills of Nepal. Hence, it is justified that there is an immediate need of conducting research on existing production, value addition, income contribution and marketing situation of cash crop and having clear understanding of factors that affect rural poor farmer's decision on growing and sustainable management of high value cash crops.

1.4 Objectives

The overall objective of the study was to analyze the production economics and marketing performance of coffee in Parbat District of Nepal. The specific objectives were;

- To analyze gross margin, benefit cost ratio and factors affecting in coffee production.
- To analyze the contribution of coffee in household income.
- To identify and rank the problems associated with production and marketing of Coffee.
- To identify marketing channel used in the trade of Coffee.

1.5 Scope and limitation of the study

This study is an attempt to analyze the economics of coffee production along with its marketing performance. This study would furnish some kind of conclusion, recommendation and feedback, which could be useful basis for future research and also in planning, implementing and evaluating a development-oriented program for all sectors, engaged in coffee production. Despite having the great scope the research has its limitations.

Any research process will involve challenges and complications, especially when the context is foreign to the researcher (Scott *et al.,* 2006). The research was carried out mostly on recall basis, which might lead to some response errors. In addition, the research covered only a limited area and population due to resource and time constrains, which might not be generalized to other areas of the country. Because of the diversified nature of human being with respect to many aspects like intelligence, attitude, thinking, perception, status, ethnicity, family size, landholding, knowledge and the information gathered from the respondents may vary to other locations.

2 LITERATURE REVIEW

This chapter presents the brief review of the coffee production scenario worldwide, in Nepal and in Parvat district. Earlier studies carried out on cost of coffee production, gross margin, production function analysis of coffee production and problems regarding coffee production and marketing are studied under this chapter.

2.1 Coffee in Nepal

Coffee is a high value cash crop with environmental importance, and is being popular among Nepalese people since last few decades. Historically, it is believed that a saint named Hira Giri in Aanpchaur, Gulmi district, introduced coffee for the first time in Nepal from Myanmar in 1944 (Bastola, 2007). Presently, coffee is cultivated in around 40 districts, but it has been producing commercially in about 20-22 hill districts in Nepal.

As the climate and soil in the mid and high hills of Nepal are found to be very suitable for *Arabica* coffee, the coffee planted in Nepal is all *Arabica* (Giri, 2006). Coffee industry is in rudimentary stage in Nepal but have high potential. Coffee farming in Nepal is proven as promising due to the availability of soil with fragile nature and appropriate climate in the mid hill (Nepal, 2006). Coffee is being growing in Nepal from low to mid hills (800-1600 masl) covering about 21,000 ha. NTCDB (2014) estimated that coffee production engages around 27 thousand farm families. Despite the hurdles, the expansion of total coffee cultivation area, production and productivity has been increased by 17, 24.36 and 6.5% respectively. About 25-30% of the domestic demand is estimated to be fulfilled by the local production (Poudel, 2003).

2.2 Worldwide Coffee production Scenario

The world coffee production is overwhelmingly dominated by Latin America and Africa accounting for as high as 80% of the total production. Rest 20 % is contributed by Asia and the Pacific region. Brazil alone produces about 35% followed by Vietnam 18%, Colombia 6%, Indonesia 6%, Ethiopia 4% and India 3% (ICO, 2006).

2.3 Coffee production in Parbat

Cultivation of shade coffee, *Arabica* variety with marketable intercrops is way of farming in Parvat. Total area and production coffee in Parbat district is 76 ha. and 10.5 metric ton respectively with approximate 1800 farmers (MoAD, 2013). Whereas; total national area, production and farmers of coffee sector is 1750 ha., 366 mt. and 27000 farmers respectively (MoAD, 2013). Its export is mainly to Japan and South Korea.

2.4 Economics of Coffee production

Poudel *et al.*, (2009) found that the fertilizer cost was among the highest cost followed by the labour cost. Total variable cost of coffee production in organic farm was found Nrs.8086.25, the gross revenue of 12205.38 and gross margin of 4119.13 Rs/farm. One hectare of coffee farm yields a net surplus of about Rs. 200,000 with paid labor and it becomes about Rs. 250,000 with family labor (Bajracharya and Pathak, 2001).

The study by Pandit (2008) on coffee in different districts of Nepal revealed that the average gross margin of coffee production in Palpa, Kavre and Syangha was 119129.70/ha, 139984.78/ha and 176173.57/ha respectively. The average total cost was found 73504.18 Rs/ha in Palpa.

The study by Bastola (2007) on coffee production found that the average variable cost of production per ropani per year was Rs.4194 while average gross return was Rs. 13093 at Rs. 25 per kg of fresh cherry with average production of 524 kg fresh cherry per ropani per year and with no production in the first two years. The gross margin of coffee production was Rs. 8899 per ropani per year. The overall B:C ratio of coffee cultivation was found to be 3.121.

The profitability of coffee production in Kabbu region of Nigeria was studied by Mohammed *et al.* (2013). The cost and return analysis shows that coffee production in the area has a profitability index of 0.29 with a return margin of N 8,855.40 per household per hectare.

2.5 Constraints of coffee production and marketing

Poudel *et al.*, (2009) in their analysis found the major problem of organic coffee production in Gulmi district were unavailability of skilled labour, Farm yard manure unavailability, insect pest ranked 1st, 2nd and 3rd respectively. Small scale of production, scattered area under coffee farming, lack of quality saplings, pests esp.

the stem borer and diseases infestations, lack of crop insurance, long gestation period, and limited functions of NTCDB are the major constraints in coffee production in Nepal (AEC, 2006).

Pandit (2008) in her study revealed that the major problems associated with the coffee production in Palpa district were Pest as Borer, followed by lack of good varieties, disease, lack of technical know-how etc. whereas the major problems faced by the farmers in Gulmi district were Pest followed by Disease and lack of good varieties, lack of irrigation etc.

Bhandari (1990) found that high yields in coffee have not benefited growers, much because of the slump in prices in the world market during 1988 and prices thrash to its lowest level in more than three decades, characterized by confusion and an uncertainty in international coffee trade. It gave an additional shock to the Indian growers to continue the coffee cultivation.

2.6 Market, marketing system and status of coffee

Marketing system includes producers, traders, transporters, wholesalers, retailers, and consumers as the main actors to carry out different activities (HMG/N, 1999). An efficient marketing system is essential for timely delivery of the product with the reduction in the cost of marketing (Pun and Karmacharya, 1998).

In the coffee sector there are only few major players in this business sharing some portion in national as well as international market such as Everest Coffee Mills (P) Ltd, Panchkhal (16%), Highland Coffee Promotion P. Ltd, Kathmandu (20%),Nepal Organic Coffee Products, Madan Pokhara (12.5%), Gulmi Sahakari Sastha (25%), Nepal Coffee Company, Butwal(12.5%), Himalaya Coffee Products (P) Ltd, Kathmandu(2%), Plantec Incorporate (7.5%), District Cooperatives Federation Ltd, Tamghas and Nepal Mountain Coffee Company, Lalitpur (ATPMC, 2004).

2.7 Institutional involvement in Coffee sector

CoPP-Helvetas, AEC, Coffee Producers Association, Nepal Tea and Coffee Development Board, Nepal Tree Crop Global Development Alliance, and Winrock International are the promoters of Nepalese coffee (Rana, 2004). Besides, Ministry of Agriculture and Cooperatives (MOAC), Nepal Agriculture Research Council (NARC), NCPA, and other private sectors are also involved in the promotion of coffee in Nepal (Bajracharya and

Pathak, 2001). There has been some degree of efforts from government and non-government sectors to support the coffee sub-sector by motivating farmers to grow coffee. Local Initiatives Support Program (LISP) and Sustainable Soil Management Program (SSMP) under Helvetas–Nepal have been implementing coffee related activities in Palpa, Syangja, Parbat, Kavre and Sindhupalchowk districts. Few development organizations and projects like Gulmi–Arghakhanchi Rural Development Project (GARDP), Winrock International, DANIDA, etc. are promoting coffee for crop diversification and income generation, contributing to the expansion of the coffee production area (CoPP, 2003).

3 RESEARCH METHODOLOGY

This section includes different methodological framework for research procedure which consists of four main sub-sections. The first section describes the conceptual framework of the study. Second section describes the sampling procedure, sample frame, sample size and survey design. Third section describes data collection procedure and data analysis techniques are described in detail in the fourth section.

3.1 Selection of the study area

Pakuwa VDC of Parbat District of Nepal was selected for the study. Parbat District is a mid hill district of Western Development Region of Nepal lies between $28^0 00'19''$North- $28^0 23'59''$North latitudes and $83^0 33'40''$East- $83^0 49'30''$East 'longitudes with total area of 536.86 sq. Km (DADO, 2013). Out of the cultivated land only 11.96% is under year-round irrigation and 4.94% is seasonal irrigation. The average land holding of the district is 0.8 hectare per family. A total area of 59 ha is under coffee farming which is increased by 25.53% and total production of 12tons of coffee out of which Pakuwa VDC comprise 5 tons of production.

The reasons for purposive selection of the VDC are involvement of most of the farmers in coffee plantation from long time, from market modality perspective and the researcher's accessibility.

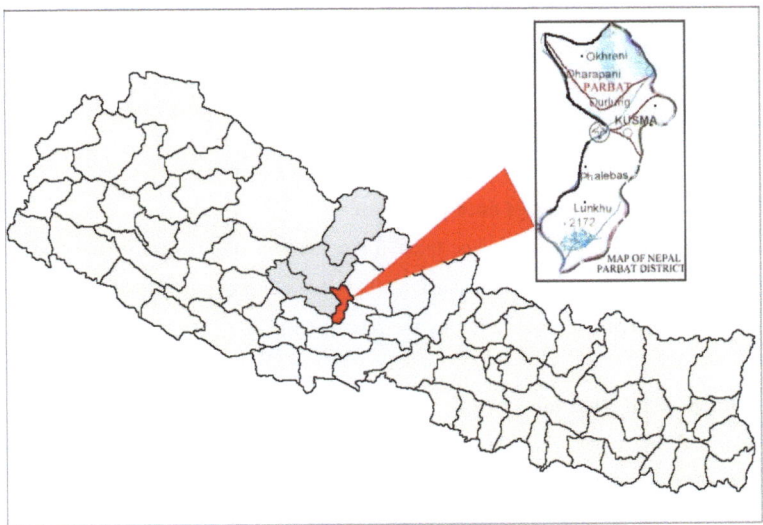

Figure 1. Map of Nepal showing Parbat District (Research site)

3.2 Sampling procedure and selection of the respondent

The size of the sample and amount of variation, usually affect the quantity and quality of information obtained from the survey. Using appropriate sampling methods, both factors can be controlled (Scheaffer, 1979).

3.2.1 Sampling method

Sampling theory provides an opportunity to minimize cost and to achieve acceptable results (Casley and Kumar, 1988). However, a sampling procedure involves the following steps: defining the population, sample frame, sample size and sample selection procedure.

3.2.2 Defining the population

The coffee farmers of Pakuwa VDC in Parvat district who have long experience in coffee production were taken as the sample population for this study.

3.2.3 Sampling frame, sample size and sample selection procedure

The sampling frame was prepared with the Key informants of the respective District and VDC. Yearlong coffee producers in Pakuwa VDC of Parvat district constitute the sampling frame for this study. Total sample of 40 farmers cultivating coffee were selected randomly for the study.

The best way to avoid bias in the sample selection process is use of simple random sampling in which each unit of the population has an equal chance for selection (Scheaffer, 1979). Thus by using sampling frame, a simple random sampling procedure was used to collect necessary information.

3.3 Methods and techniques of data collection

Various sources and technique were used for collection of necessary information. The methodologies consisted of field survey, review of previous studies, focus group discussion and also direct observation by the researchers.

3.3.1 Sources of information

The pre-tested interview schedule was administered to the respondents to collect primary information. All randomly selected participants were visited and interviewed. Primary data were also collected through Focus Group Discussion (FGD). Secondary information were collected from the various published materials like bulletins, books, journals, research articles, publications from district offices of respected site, proceedings of various NGOs and INGOs, reports of District Agriculture Development Office (DADO), reports from the Ministry of Agriculture and Development (MoAD), reports of District coffee producers association (DCPA), publications of National Tea and Coffee Development Board (NTCDB), Coffee Cooperatives etc.

3.4 Survey design and data collection procedure

3.4.1 Reconnaissance Survey

It was a informal survey on which the researcher himself carried out a field visit of the study area with the objective to become familiar with different features of the study area such as the geography, local community, government organization and non- government organization etc.

3.4.2 Interview schedule design

Interview schedule was prepared for the collection of information from the selected respondents. Different questions regarding the family size, land availability, source of income, coffee production and sales, cost of coffee production, problems of coffee production and marketing and marketing channel in trade of coffee etc. were collected by using interview schedule.

3.4.3 Pre-testing of interview schedule

The interview schedule and checklist was pre-tested in a nearby VDC with 6 farmers from Archale VDC, prior to administering to the actual respondents. Necessary modifications were made and the schedule was revised and put in the final form.

3.4.4 Field survey

The field survey was conducted as far as convenient. The respondents were interviewed by visiting their homes. The field survey was done during June 10-20, 2014. The questions were in English but were asked in the local languages to the respondents. Regular checking and validation of the information was done immediately after filling the interview schedule.

3.5 Methods and techniques of data analysis

After collection of necessary information it was coded and entered to computer for analysis. Data was fed and analysis was done by using statistical packages for social sciences (SPSS V.16) and STATA 12. Mean, standard deviations, frequency, percentage etc. were used to derive inference needed.

3.5.1 Quantitative data analysis

Quantitative data were analyzed by using the both descriptive and analytical statistics.

3.5.1.1 Descriptive analysis

Socioeconomic and farm characteristics of the respondents like family size, age, gender, caste, occupational pattern, land holding size, economically active population etc. were described using simple descriptive statistics like frequency count, percentage, mean, standard deviation etc.

3.6 Economics of coffee production

This section examines the economics of coffee production of sampled farmers with specific focus on costs, yields, returns and profits. Important variable costs items were taken under study and to make comparisons more scientific prevailing market price was used for each input and also for price of output.

3.6.1 Cost of coffee production

In this study only variable cost items were included for analyzing the cost of coffee production. The variable cost included were cost of sapling, cost of labor, cost of manure, cost of plant protection, cost on irrigation, cost on harvesting and marketing. Total variable cost was calculated by summing all the variable cost items.

Cost of coffee production (Rs.) = $C_{plant} + C_{labor} + C_{manure} + C_{pesticide} + C_{other}$

Where,

C_{plant} (Rs.) = Cost of plant/sapling

C_{labor} (Rs.) = Cost of labor used

C_{manure} (Rs.) = Cost of FYM/organic manure used

$C_{pesticide}$ (Rs.) = Expenditure on plant protection materials

C_{other} (Rs.) = Other cost on coffee production including cost on irrigation, cost on marketing, cost on postharvest etc.

3.6.2 Gross margin, profitability and cost-benefit analysis

This is the difference between the Gross Farm Income (GFI) and the Total Variable Cost (TVC). It is a useful planning tool in situations where fixed capital is negligible portion of the farming enterprise in the case of small scale subsistence agriculture (Olukosi and Erhabor, 1988).

Gross margin was calculated as:

GM= GFI-TVC

Gross Margin (Rs.) = Gross return (Rs.) - Total variable cost (Rs.)

Where, Gross return(Rs.) = Price of fresh cherry (Rs./Kg)× total quantity sold (Kg.)

Total variable cost (Rs.) = Summation of cost on all variable input.

Profitability index= Net farm Income (NFI) / TVC

Similarly, benefit cost analysis was done using the total cost and gross return from the French bean farming. Cost of production was calculated by summing all the variable cost items in the production process. For calculating gross return, income from the sale was accounted. Thus the benefit cost analysis was carried out by using formula;

$$B/C\ ratio = \frac{Gross\ return\ (NRs.)}{Total\ variable\ cost\ (NRs.)}$$

3.6.3 Production function analysis

The Cobb-Douglas type of production was used in this study as it is the most widely used in the agricultural research and is convenient for the comparison of the partial elasticity coefficient (Prajneshu, 2008). The following form of Cobb- Douglas production function was used to determine the contribution of different factors on production and to estimate the efficiency of the variable factors of production of coffee.

$Y = aX_1^{b1} X_2^{b2} X_3^{b3} X_4^{b4} X_5^{b5} e^u$

Where,

Y= Gross Income (Rs./ha.)

X_1= Labor cost (Rs./ ha.)

X_2= Cost of manure (Rs./ ha.)

X_3= Cost of sapling/plant (Rs./ ha.)

X_4= Number of productive plants (Number)

X_5= Area under coffee (ha.)

u = Random disturbance term, b_1 ...b_4 are the coefficient to be estimated.

The Cobb- Douglas production function in the form expressed above was linearised in to a logarithmic function with a view to getting a form amenable to practical purposes as expresses below.

$$lnY = lna + b1lnX1 + b2lnX2 + b3lnX3 + b4lnX4 + b5lnX5 + u$$

Where,

ln= Natural logarithm,   a= constant,   u= Error term

3.6.4 Return to Scale Analysis

This is the measure of farm success in producing maximum output from a given set of inputs. For the calculation of return to scale from coffee, Cobb-Douglas production function was used and calculated using formula;

$$RTS = \sum b_i,$$

Where, b_i =regression coefficient of ith variables.

Return to Scale decision rule:

RTS<1: Decreasing return to scale

RTS=1: Constant return to scale

RTS>1: Increasing return to scale

3.7 Contribution of coffee production in household income

The percentage share of coffee in the total household income was analyzed. Average income from coffee, income from cereals, income from vegetables, income from livestock and off-farm income were taken and percentage share of these sectors to the average household income was calculated. Thus, total household income was;

$$Yi = X1 + X2 + X3 + X4 + X5$$

Where,

Yi = total household income (100%)

X1 = income from coffee (%),

X2 = income from cereals (%),

X3 = income from vegetables (%),

X4 = income from livestock (%),

X5= off-farm income (%)

3.8 Analysis of problems associated with production and marketing of Coffee

Various problems regarding production and marketing were analyzed through scaling techniques. A respondent was asked to choose various categories indicating different strength of agreement and disagreement. The categories are scored and his total score measures respondent's attitude, which is the sum of the scores of the categories. Thus, each response is given a numerical score and the total score of a respondent is found by summing up his different scores for different responses. This total score indicates position in the continuum (Miah, 1993). The index of severity was computed by using the following formula:

$$I_{severity} = \sum S_i f_i / N$$

Where,

I = index $0 < I < 1$

S_i = scale value at ith severity

f_i = frequency of the ith severity

N = total number of respondents = $\sum f_i$

4 RESULTS AND DISCUSSION

This chapter deals with the results obtained through the analysis of collected information and data. The discussions of the results are outlined under the following subheadings.

4.1 Socio-economic and demographic information

The socio-economic characteristics of respondents include age distribution, population and sex distribution, economically active population, education, involvement of farmers in co-operative, group, access to credit etc. These characteristics are described below.

4.1.1 Age distribution of respondents and household head

Age is one of the most important factors pertaining to the individual's personality make up, since the needs and the way in which an individual thinks are closely related to the number of years a person lived. The average age of the respondent was 48.97 years ranging from 18 to 78 years. Whereas; the average age of the household head was 56.50 years ranging from 26 years to 87 years (Table 1).

Table 1. Age distribution of respondents and household head in the study area (2014)

Characteristics	Age of respondents (years)	Age of Household head (years)
Minimum age	18	26
Maximum age	78	87
Mean age	48.97	56.50

4.1.2 Family type and family size

Among the respondent 72.5 percent were male. The average family size of the study area was 6.42 with per household average male 3.37 and average female 3.00 (Table 2)

Table 2. Distribution of the population by sex in the study area (2014)

Characteristics	Frequency	Percentage
Male	29	72.5
Female	11	27.5
Total	40	100
Average male (Number/household)	3.37	-
Average female (Number/household)	3.00	-
Average family size (Number/household)	6.42	-

The household were found as patriarchal, out of the 40 households that were sampled in area 72.5 % was male headed family remaining only 27.5 % were only the female headed family (Table 3)

Table 3. Sex distribution of the household head in the study area (2014)

Characteristics	Male Headed	Female Headed	Total
Frequency	29	11	40
Percentage	72.5	27.5	100

In the study area most of the families were nuclear type. Nuclear family consists of the 70.0 percent and remaining 30.0 percent was the joint family type (Figure 2).

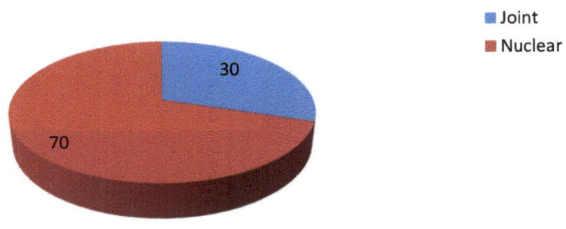

Figure 2. Family type of the respondents in the study area (2014)

4.1.3 Ethnicity of the respondents

The study revealed that the majority of the population was *Brahmin/ Chettri* (75.0%) followed by *Aadibasi/Janajati* (15.0%) and *Dalit* (10.0%) as shown on Table 4 below.

Table 4. Ethnic composition of respondents in study area (2014)

Ethnicity	Frequency	Percent
Brahmin/Chettri	30	75
Aadibasi/Janajati	6	15
Dalit	4	10
Total	40	100

4.1.4 Age distribution of the sampled population and their major occupation.

The sampled population was categorized into three different age groups in which economically active population referred to the population belonging to the age group 16 to 59 years (GoN). Study resulted that, 58.36% of population was economically active and among the economically active population agriculture was the major occupation for 80% (Table 5).

Table 5. Age distribution of the sampled population in the study area (2014)

	Age Distribution		Major Occupation	
Age Group	Frequency	Percentage	Agriculture(%)	Non-agriculture(%)
<15 years	67	26.07	–	–
16-59 years	150	58.36	80	20
>60	40	15.57	–	–
Total	257	100		

4.1.5 Educational status of sampled households

The majority of the population under sampled household have the secondary level of education (40.0%) followed by the higher secondary education (25.0%). Illiteracy rate in the study area was 17.5% (Figure 3).

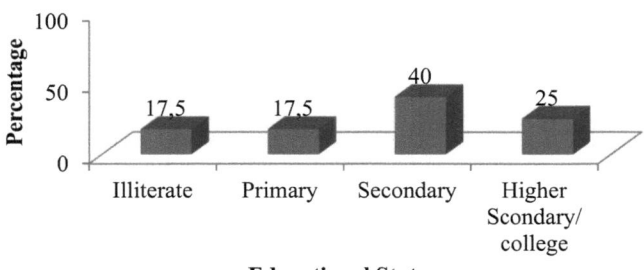

Educational Status

Figure 3. Educational status of sampled household in the study area (2014)

4.2 Farm characteristics

4.2.1 Land holding characteristics

Table 6. Farm characteristics of the respondents in the study area (2014)

Land	Mean	SE
Area under coffee	0.13	0.02
Total owned area	0.75	0.07
Area under irrigation	0.55	0.05

To establish the characteristics of land of study area it was categorized as total area owned, area under coffee cultivation and area under irrigation. Average size of total area of study size was 0.75ha.Of which coffee cultivated area was 0.13ha. Similarly area under irrigation was 0.55ha. (Table 6).

4.3 Institutional characteristics

4.3.1 Organizational participation and Access of credit

This refers to degree of participation or involvement of respondent in cooperative as member. The coffee growing farmers were mainly involved in the co-operatives. Below table shows, out of 40 respondent, 62.5 % of sampled household head were participated in cooperative named *Pragati coffee shakari sanstha* and remaining 37.5% of household head were not formally participated (Table 7).

Table 7. Organizational participation of Coffee growers in the study area (2014)

Cooperative member	Frequency	Percent	Access to credit	Frequency	Percent
Membership	25	62.5	Yes	32	80.0
Non-membership	15	37.5	No	8	20.0
Total	40	100.0	Total	40	100.0

Credit is the major factor for the production of any of the crops. The credit facilities for the people involved in coffee farming were provided by the local co-operatives in the study area and also by the banks. It was found that the majority of (80%) of household lack credit support and only 20% have access to it in the study area among coffee farmers.

4.3.2 Participation on trainings

Training is the important tool for the better farming practice. Most of the institutions and organizations as well as other business agencies working for promotion of coffee in the country have given utmost importance in training on quality production, quality processing and efficient marketing aspects.

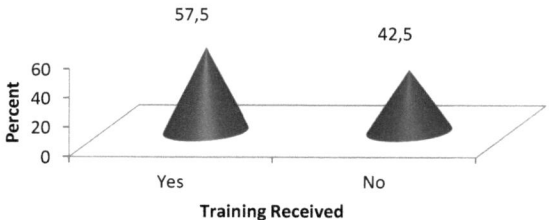

Figure 4. Training received situation among sampled households in the study area (2014)

As far as the participation of farmers in commercial production and processing of related trainings was concerned, 57.5% of respondent had received training and 42.5% of respondent hadn't received any of the training related to it (Figure 4). This resemble the more than half of sample respondent been motivate through training.

4.4 Production economics of Coffee

4.4.1 Contribution of coffee in household income

The average income from the different sources is shown in the table 13. Table revealed that overall contribution of coffee to household income was 16.26 percent. It can be concluded that 16.26 percent contribution to the household income from a single crop was a good sign for its commercialization. Income from coffee could be raised and it could be an important source of household income. Further, vegetable, livestock and cereal crops contributes 16.05, 18.19 and 7.43 percent respectively (Table 8).

Table 8. Major source of household income in the study area (2014)

Particulars (Rs.)	Average income	Percentage contribution
Annual income from Coffee	22733.7	16.26*
Annual income from cereals	10395.3	7.43
Annual income from vegetables	22428.5	16.05
Annual income from livestock and livestock products	25428.5	18.19
Annual income from off farm and other sources	58825.0	42.07
Annual household income	139816.8	100.00

* More than 10% contribution in household income shows good sign of commercialization.

4.4.2 Gross margin, profitability index and benefit-cost analysis on coffee production

Table 9 revealed that the average total cost per hectare of coffee production was NRs. 73253.50 whereas; per hectare return from coffee production was NRs. 163458.93. From the analysis, it could be seen that per ha average gross margin was NRs. 90205.43 with benefit-cost ratio 3.84. Similar to this result, the gross margin on coffee production was found 119129.70/ha in Palpa district (Pandit, 2008). However, greater than 1 benefit cost ratio in the study area also indicated that coffee cultivation was running in profit. The result further showed that the profitability index was 1.23. This indicates that coffee farmers in the study area earned Rs. 1.23 on each rupees invested in production process.

Table 9. Gross margin, profitability and benefit-cost from coffee in the study area (2014)

Statistics	Mean	Std. Error
Total cost/hectare	73253.50	6624.71
Total return/hectare	163458.93	6138.43
Gross margin/hectare	90205.43	10935.29
B:C Ratio	3.84	0.63

Profitability Index= 90205/73253.50= 1.23

4.4.3 Factors affecting the production of coffee

Table 10 resulted that the number of productive plant was the most significant factor affecting production of coffee in Parvat. The output elasticity of number of productive plant was 0.894 indicating that holding the other explanatory variables constant, one percent change in number of productive plant contributed 0.894 percent increase in output. Also, the cost on sapling/plant was significant and 1 percent increased in cost of sapling contributed 0.151 percent increased in the output of coffee.

Table 10. Estimated coefficients for the factors affecting production of coffee in the study area (2014)

Variables	Coefficient	Std. Error	t-value	P>|t|
Constant	.145	1.047	0.14	0.891
Number of productive plant	.894	.072	12.37 ***	0.000
Area under coffee cultivation	-.058	.052	-1.12	0.271
Labor	.417	.282	1.48	0.149
Manure	-.289	.247	-1.17	0.251
Sapling	.151	.067	2.25 **	0.031
R^2	0.963			
F-value	180.67			
Return to Scale ($\sum bi$)	1.26			

*** Significant at 1% level

** Significant at 5% level

4.4.4 Return to Scale

Return to scale was calculated as the sum of individual production inputs elasticities. Return to scale described response of an output toward its proportional change from input in overall. The elasticity of production which is the sum of coefficients of the Cobb-Douglas production function is the return to scale. The summation of all the values of parameter was 1.26, which indicated the increasing returns to scale means that all input addition by one percent would increase output by 1.26 percent.

4.5 Reasons for the cultivation of coffee

From the table below, it can be concluded that more income ranked as the top priority reason for the cultivation of coffee with index value 0.87 followed by easy to sell, high quality of produced, high demand and price, organizational support, utilization of marginal land respectively (Table 11).

Table 11. Reasons for the cultivation of coffee in the study area (2014)

Reasons	1	0.8	0.6	0.4	0.2	0	Index	Rank
More Income	21	13	5	1	0	0	0.87	I
Easy to sell	11	17	9	2	1	0	0.775	II
High Quality of produced	5	8	13	13	1	0	0.615	III
High demand and price	3	2	2	16	15	2	0.38	IV
Organizational support	0	0	0	3	12	25	0.09	VI
Utilization of marginalized land	0	0	11	5	11	13	0.27	V

4.6 Constraints in production and marketing of Coffee

Table 12. Constraints in production and marketing of coffee in the study area (2014)

Problems on Production	Index	Rank	Problem on Marketing	Index	Rank
lack of irrigation	0.93	I	Low price	0.81	I
lack of knowledge	0.75	II	Lack of Processing	0.43	II
Disease and pest incident	0.41	II	Lack of organized market	0.59	III
lack of skilled manpower	0.75	III	Lack of Market information	0.56	IV
Unavailability of labor	0.64	IV	No certification	0.60	V
lack of quality sampling	0.6	V	Transportation	0.94	VI
Poor soil fertility status	0.31	VI	low production	0.27	VII
lack of crop insurance	0.19	VII	low Quality production	0.36	VIII

Table 12 above resulted that the major problems hindering the coffee production in the study area was lack of irrigation which was ranked as most severe in the study area with index value 0.93 followed by lack of knowledge, lack of skilled manpower, labor unavailability, lack of quality sapling and lastly poor soil fertility status and lack of crop insurance. Whereas; low price of coffee was ranked as most severe marketing constraints in coffee with index value 0.94 followed by lack of processing, lack of organized market, lack of market information, no certification, transportation and low production (Table 12).

4.7 Marketing system and Marketing Channel of coffee

Coffee marketing encompasses all activities performed in moving coffee of different forms; include producers, Pulper operators, DCPA, processors and exporters and retailers which are major actors of coffee marketing in Nepal.

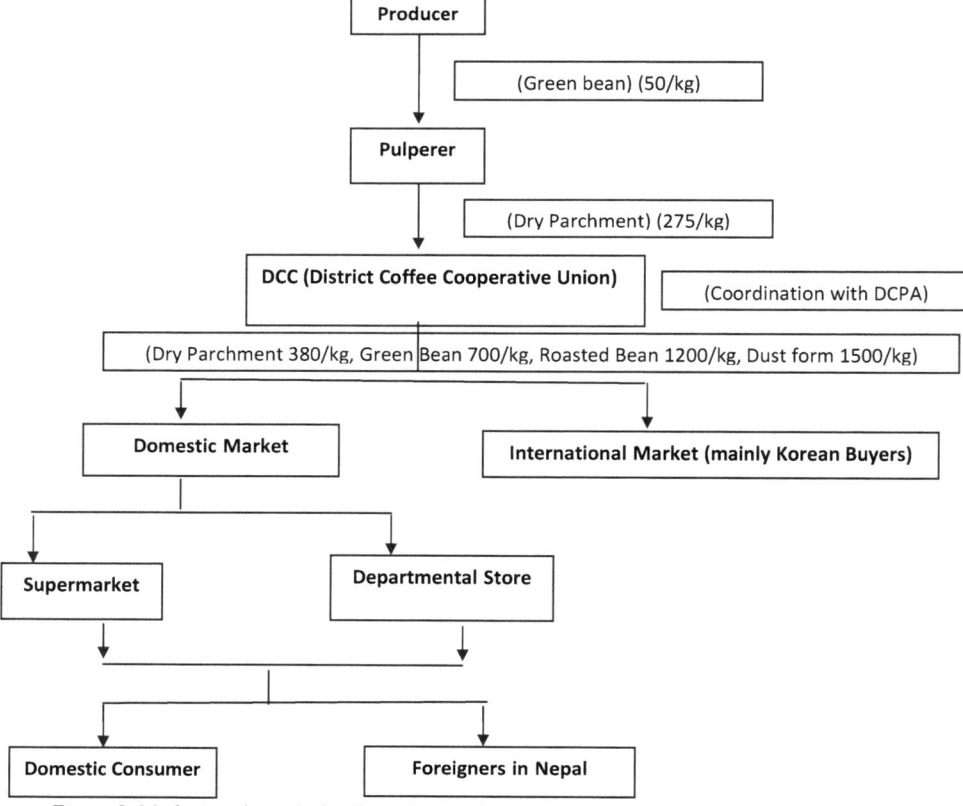

Figure 5. Marketing channel of coffee in Parvat district (2014)

In Parvat, firstly the producers sell fresh cherries to Pulper operator in the locality. Fresh cherries are depulped, fermented, washed and dried to form dry parchment. Dry parchment are packed in sacs and is collected by DCC in district headquarter. DCC in coordination with DCPA sold dry parchment, green beans, roasted bean to domestic and international market (Figure 5).

5 SUMMARY AND CONCLUSION

This chapter deals with the summary of the whole study and conclusion derived from the findings. Some suggestions for future program implementations and research are also presented hereunder.

5.1 Summary

Coffee beings one of potential and a commercial crop in the hilly districts of mid-hill regions of Nepal as being suitable climatic and soil condition. This research tried to find out the production economics and marketing performance of coffee in Parvat district of Nepal. The specific objectives were to analyze gross margin, benefit cost ratio and factors affecting in coffee production, analyze the contribution of coffee in household income, identify and rank the problems associated with production and marketing of Coffee and to identify marketing channel used in the trade of Coffee in Parvat district.

Altogether 40 coffee farmers were selected randomly for the study. Primary data were collected through pre-tested interview schedule, focus group discussion and direct observation methods. Descriptive statistics, cost benefit analysis, Cobb-Douglas production function regression model and indexing techniques were used for the analysis of the data.

Study resulted that the average age of the respondent was 48.97 and that of household head was 56.50 years. Among the respondents 72.5 percent were male. The average family size of the study area was 6.42 with average male 3.37 and average female 3.00. Out of the 40 households that were sampled in area 72.5 % was male headed family. Nuclear type of family consists of the 70.0 percent and remaining 30.0 percent was the joint family type. The majority of the population were *Brahmin/ Chettri* (75.0%) followed by *Aadibasi/Janajati* (15.0%) and *Dalit* (10.0%). About 58 % of population was economically active and among the economically active population agriculture was the major occupation for 80%. The majority of the population under sampled household have the secondary level of education (40.0%) followed by the higher secondary education (25.0%). Illiteracy rate in the study area was 17.5%. Average area owned by respondents' was 0.75ha. of which mean area under coffee was 0.13ha. Similarly, area under irrigation was 0.55ha. About 62.5 % of sampled household head were participated in cooperative named *Pragati coffee shakari sanstha*. Majority (80%) of household lack credit support and 57.5% of respondent had received training related to coffee.

Overall contribution of coffee to household income was 16.26 percent. It can be concluded that 16.26 percent contribution to the household income from a single crop was a good sign for its commercialization. Per hectare average gross margin from coffee was NRs. 90205.43 with benefit-cost ratio 3.84. The highest benefit cost ratio indicated that coffee cultivation was prominently profitable enterprise in Parbat. However, greater than 1 benefit cost ratio in the study area also indicated that coffee cultivation was running in profit. The result further showed that the profitability index was 1.23. This indicates that coffee farmers in the study area earned Rs. 1.23 on each rupees invested in production process. Number of productive plant and cost of sapling/plant materials were the most significant factor affecting production of coffee in Parvat and holding the other explanatory variables constant, one percent change in number of productive plant contributed 0.894 percent and 0.151 percent increase in output respectively. Increasing returns to scale was observed that all input addition by one percent would increase output by 1.26 percent. More income from coffee ranked as the top priority reason for the cultivation of coffee. The major problems hindering the coffee production in the study area was lack of irrigation which was ranked as most severe in the study area whereas; low price of coffee was ranked as most severe marketing constraints in coffee.

In Parvat, firstly the producers sell fresh cherries to Pulper operator in the locality. Fresh cherries are depulped, fermented, washed and dried to form dry parchment. Dry parchment are packed in sacs and is collected by DCC in district headquarter. DCC in coordination with DCPA sold dry parchment, green beans, roasted bean to domestic and international market. The major stakeholders of coffee marketing in Parbat are the producers, pulper operators, DCC under DCPA, domestic and international market.

5.2 Conclusion

Parvat district is with immense potentialities for coffee business in Nepal. Farmers are eagerly increasing area under coffee cultivation each year and consequently. High gross margin, increase return to scale, benefit-cost ratio and more than one profitability index on coffee production in the study area showed that coffee cultivation is best suitable enterprise for income generation. Reasons more income and easy to sell were stand for the coffee cultivation which shows future involvement of majority of farmers if irrigation facility will be provided as ,lack of irrigation was found as the most hindering factor. Also, package trainings on improved technology and organic disease pest management techniques should be given frequently. Coffee sapling and numbers of productive plants were found most significant factors in the income, such that good variety and quality of sapling should be provided and farmers should done plantation based on scientific methods. Price fixation and stabilization along with establishment of well organized market will be done from Government level to overcome marketing problems in the study area. The major stakeholders of coffee marketing in Parbat are the producers, pulper operators, DCC under DCPA, domestic and international market. Thus, the study resulted positive economic significance of coffee and this shows immense need of Government, NGOs, traders, and other line agencies to lay efforts on production and marketing management such that its production and income can be raised.

5.3 Recommendations

Based on the study about production economics and marketing performance of coffee, following recommendations are made for the farmer, government sector, other organizations and researchers.

- Plantations area was not systematically and scientifically managed and that reducing the yield and income, so capacity building of farmers is suggested.
- Suggestions for the researcher to identify the organic pest control mechanism. Also, Government and other research stations should focus on the commodity specific pest management research.
- Coffee production is profitable, so investment agencies can invest in this sector.
- Package trainings program on improved technology and organic disease pest management techniques should be implemented.
- The net profit was found minimum that renders the farmers to plant the coffee, government should give subsidies on the materials and better price of the product may enhance the business.
- The major of the problem faced by the farmers was of irrigation and low price. Such that Government as well as other institutes working in this sector should implement the program to address these issues.

5.4 Areas for further research

- Projection of domestic and international demand of Nepalese coffee in future.
- Profitability of shade as companion crop and effect on coffee disease and pest.
- Research on insect pest disease dynamics and control.
- Study on processing technology and quality improvement.
- Effect of climate change on coffee production and contribution to food security.

LITERATURE CITED

AEC. 2006. Coffee. Agro Enterprise Center/Federation of Nepalese Chambers of Commerce and Industry, Kathmandu, Nepal.

APP. 1995. Agriculture Perspective Plan Nepal.Agricultural Projects Services Centre, Kathmandu and John Mellor Associates, Inc.Washington D.C.

Bajracharya, P. 2003. Business Plan for HCPC Limited, AEC/FNCCI. Katmandu. Nepal.

Bajracharya, P. and K.P. Pathak. 2001. An Assessment of Coffee Potential in Nepal. Swiss Agency for Development and Cooperation. pp. 1-13.

Bastola, U. 2007. Economics of Coffee Production, Processing and Marketing in Nepal. M. Sc. Thesis. Tribhuvan University. Institute of Agriculture and Animal Science, Rampur.

Bhandari, A. 1990. Coffee: Hard choice a head. The Hindu Survey of Indian Agriculture, 3: 68-69.

Casely, D. and K. Kumar. 1988. The Collection Analysis and Use of Monitoring and Evaluation Data. Baltimore, The Hohns Hopkins University Press.

CoPP. 2003. Coffee Sector in Nepal: Constraints and Opportunities for Sustainability. Coffee Promotion Project, Helvetas – Nepal.

DADO Parvat. 2013. Annual Agriculture Development Program and Statistical Bulletin. District Agriculture Development Office, Parvat.

Dhakal, B.R. 2004. Coffee Manual. National Tea and Coffee Development Board, New Baneshor, Kathmandu, Nepal.

Giri, Y.P. 2006. Status and Potentiality of Coffee Cultivation in Nepal. In: Tea-A-Tea. National Tea and Coffee Development Board, New Baneshwor, Kathmandu, Nepal.

HMG/N. 1999. A Study on Mandarin Orange Marketing: A Case Study of Tanahun and Syangja District. Marketing Development Division, Harihar Bhawan, Kathmandu.

ICO. 2006. Coffee: Botanical Aspects. International Coffee Organization. (Retrieved on 15. August 2014).

Khanal, D. 2003. Coffee Production Technology. Bagbani Wadi. Horticulture Center, Kritipur, Nepal. Year 3. Issue 8.

Miah, A.Q. 1993. Applied statistics: A course handbook for human settlements planning. Asian Institute of Technology, Division of Human Settlements Development, Bangkok, Thailand. pp. 316-318.

MoAD. 2013. Statistical information on Nepalese agriculture 2010/2011. Ministry of Agriculture and Development. Agri-Business Promotion and Statistics Division (ABPSD), Kathmandu, Nepal.

Mohammed A.B., A.F. Ayanlere and C.M. Ekenta. 2013. Profitability of coffee production in Kabba/Bunu local government area of Kogi State Nigeria. Kabba College of Agriculture, Division of Agricultural Colleges, Ahmadu Bello University, Kabba Campus, Kogi State, Nigeria. Retrieved on 18th July 2014.

Nepal, A. 2006. Soil nutrient analysis of organic coffee farm in Gulmi district. Journal of Himalayan College of Agricultural Sciences and Technology, Green Field. Jan – Jun 2006, Vol 4, Issue 1. pp. 104-105.

NTCDB. 2014. Nepal tea and coffee development board. Retrieved on July 2014.

Olukosi, J.O. and P.O. Erhabo. 1988. Introduction to farm management economics: principles and applications.Agitab Publishers Ltd. Zaria.

Pandit, J. 2008. Export potentiality of organic coffee production in Nepal. Msc. Thesis, IAAS, Rampur.

Poudel, K.L. 2003. Report on Market Competitiveness Study of Nepalese coffee. Agro Enterprise Center/Federation of Nepalese Chambers of Commerce and Industry, Kathmandu, Nepal.

Poudel, K.L., A.P. Nepal., B. Dhungana., Y. Sugimoto., N. Yamamoto and A. Nishiwaki. 2009 .Capital Budgeting Analysis of Organic Coffee Production in Gulmi District of Nepal. University of Miyazaki. Faculty of Agriculture. Department of Environment and Resource Sciences, Interdisciplinary Graduate School for Agriculture and Engineering. Laboratory of Agricultural Economics.

Prajneshu, 2008. Fitting of Cobb-Douglas production functions: Revisited. Agricultural Economics Research Review. 21: 289-292.

Pun, L. and B.B. Karmacharya. 1988. Trainer's Manual on Vegetable. Manpower Development Agriculture Project, Kathmandu.

Rana, M.R.L. 2004. Prospects of Nepalese Coffee and its Markets. Research Project Submitted to School of Management, Kathmandu University and Agro-enterprise Centre.

Scott, S.F. Miller and K.L loyd. 2006. Doing Fieldwork in Development Geography: Research Culture and Research Spaces in Vietnam. Geographical Research. 44: 28-40.

Scheaffer, R. 1979. Elementary Survey Sampling.Massachusetts, USA, Duxbury Press.